About the Author

Paul Goska considers himself a listener more than a writer. Paul listens to the non-verbal stories in this world and writes them down to share with others. The world tells us wonderful stories if only we slow down long enough to hear them.

The Dog that Wanted to be a Bird

Paul Goska

The Dog that Wanted to be a Bird

Nightingale Books

NIGHTINGALE PAPERBACK

A CIP catalogue record for this title is
available from the British Library.
ISBN 9781838751470

Nightingale Books is an imprint of
Pegasus Elliot MacKenzie Publishers Ltd.
www.pegasuspublishers.com

First Published in 2021
Nightingale Books
Sheraton House Castle Park
Cambridge England
Printed & Bound in Great Britain

Dedication

To my family:
Charlotte, Jessica and Sophie Goska.

Pearl was a dog. A Catahoula leopard dog to be exact. Pearl was a gentle giant, a big dog with an even bigger heart.

Pearl would sit at the end of her driveway for hours and watch the birds. She stared at the birds in the trees. When they flew overhead, she chased them around the yard.

Birds fascinated Pearl. Pearl could only run in her yard. Birds could run like Pearl but they could also fly away. Pearl was envious.

One day Pearl was walking with her family when a goose flew overhead. Pearl immediately looked up at the goose and wagged her tail. "I want to be a bird," Pearl said. "I want to be able to fly."

"But why?" asked the bird. "Why do you want to be a bird when you already have so much to be thankful for being a dog?"

"I want to soar above the trees and float on the wind like you do," Pearl replied. "I want to fly away and see things no one else sees."

"But, but, but," thought the goose. "You chase sticks and walk with your family. And you get belly rubs. No one rubs my belly," sighed the goose.

"No one likes it when I bark early in the morning," Pearl said. "Everyone yells at me and tells me to be quiet. But everyone loves listening to you sing. They say you're beautiful."

"You protect your family," said the goose. "Your bark alerts them to danger. That's important."

ZOO

GIRAFFE

"But you can do things and see things no one else can and that makes you special," Pearl said. "You can fly high, and fast, and far. I want to be special too, like you."

"You get to sleep on a bed and lie on a couch. That's special. And you get fed every day. I have to find for my own food," said the goose. "That makes you special and loved."

Pearl thought about what goose said and picked up a stick. The stick was too big for Pearl's mouth, but she carried it with her anyway. She was happy because she felt special and loved.

When Pearl finished her walk, she no longer wanted to be a bird. She was content being who she was.

"Who loves you?" Pearl asked the goose.

"No one," sighed the goose.

Pearl looked up at the goose again and wagged her tail. "I love you," she said.

"That makes you special and loved, just like me."